FAMOUS INVENTORS

Douglas McTavish

Wayland

Famous people

Famous Artists
Famous Campaigners for Change
Famous Explorers
Famous Inventors
Famous Musicians
Famous Scientists

Picture acknowledgements
The publishers would like to thank the following for supplying pictures: Archiv Für Kunst und Geschichte 5, 11, 12 (lower), 15, 20; Eye Ubiquitous/Paul Seheult 42, /Tim Hawkins 44 (lower); Image Select 6, 7, 17, 34 (upper), 35; The Mansell Collection 4, 12 (upper),13; Peter Newark's Historical Pictures 18, 23, 24, 26, 44 (lower); Popperfoto 21; Science Photo Library 22, 37; Topham 16, 39, 40, 45; TRH Pictures (NASA) 32, 33, 34 (lower), 44 (upper); Wayland Picture Library *cover*, 8, 9, 10, 14 (both), 19, 25, 27, 28, 29, 30, 31, 36, 38, 41 (upper), 43; Zefa 41 (lower). Cover artwork by Peter Dennis.

Series editor: Rosemary Ashley
Book editor: Joanne Jessop
Series designer: Malcolm Walker

First published in 1993 by
Wayland (Publishers) Limited
6l Western Road, Hove
East Sussex, BN3 lJD, England

© Copyright 1993 Wayland (Publishers) Limited

British Library Cataloguing in Publication Data
McTavish, Douglas
   Famous Inventors. – (Famous People Series)
   I. Title II. Series
   609.2

ISBN 0-7502-0666-7

Typeset by Kudos Editorial and Design Services
Printed and bound in Italy by Rotolito Lombardo S.p.A, Milan

Contents

Introduction

Every tool and machine we use was invented by someone, at some time. Many, such as the wheel and the axe, were first made so long ago that the names of their inventors are lost in the past. However, later inventors are well known to us, because what they did was written about at the time.

In this book, we look at a few of the people whose inventions have changed our lives. Like most inventors, they used earlier inventions and improved or altered them. Baird, for example, could not have invented television without Marconi's earlier breakthrough in radio, while Marconi himself used the discoveries made by the German scientist Heinrich Hertz, and so on. In this way, each new invention causes a stir of interest that, in turn, leads to the development of further inventions.

Johann *Gutenberg*

Inventor of the printing press

Until the mid-fifteenth century, every single copy of a book had to be written out by hand. Most of the copying was done by monks, and each book took many months to complete. As a result, there were few books, and these were usually locked away in monastery libraries.

As a young boy in Mainz, Germany, Johann Gutenberg watched coins being made at the local mint, where his father was the Master. He was fascinated by the way the goldsmiths stamped figures and letters on to the coins. Another of his interests was watching monks at the nearby monastery slowly copying out page after page of religious scripts.

Gutenberg became a goldsmith himself, and in 1428 he moved to Strasbourg. While he was there his memory of the monks he had watched as a child may have helped him to come up with a brilliant idea – to use the techniques of metalwork to stamp, or print, words on a page in ink. If the process worked, hundreds and even thousands of copies of a book could be made quite quickly.

This old engraving shows a portrait of Gutenberg.

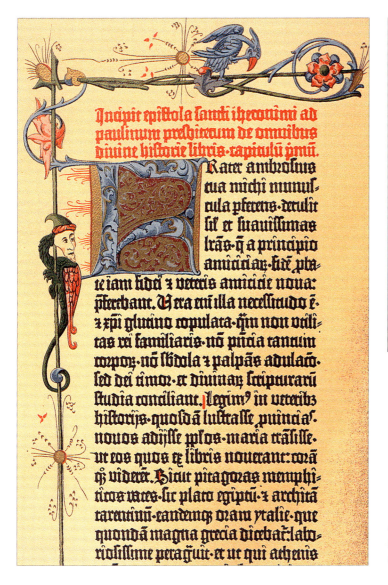

Johann Gutenberg invented the printing press. The press forced paper against metal type that had been arranged to form a page of text and then covered with ink. In 1456, three hundred copies of the Bible were produced using the press. This version of the Bible, known as the Gutenberg Bible, was the first printed book. Gutenberg's printing process led the way to all the books, newspapers and magazines we have today.

A page from the Gutenberg Bible. which was begun by Gutenberg himself and completed by Johann Fust.

Copying them out by hand would no longer be necessary.

Gutenberg's idea was to make individual letters out of so-called type metal, a mixture of the metals lead, tin and antimony. The letters were set up in a line (which included the spaces between words) called a 'type stick'. Many type sticks were fitted together in a 'forme', to make a complete page. Ink was applied to the forme, which was pressed on to a sheet of paper by a screw press. This process could be repeated to make as many

A scene in
Gutenberg's
printing shop in
the early 1450s.

copies of the page as were needed. When all the pages of a book had been printed, they were gathered and bound together inside a cover.

In 1448, Gutenberg returned to Mainz and began printing the book for which he is famous – a 1,282-page version of the Bible. However, Gutenberg was not a wealthy man, and he soon ran out of money. He formed a partnership with Johann Fust, a fellow goldsmith, who loaned him money to complete his Bible.

But Gutenberg could not repay the money he had borrowed and Fust took him to court. Fust was given Gutenberg's printing press to make up for the debt. Gutenberg lost everything. With the help of a friend he set up another printing press, but little is known of his later work and he died penniless a few years later. Meanwhile, Fust carried on printing the Gutenberg Bible, and in 1456 he completed three hundred copies. Only twenty-one of these are still in existence, and they are the most valuable printed books in the world.

Dates

1400 born in Mainz, Germany
1428 moves to Strasbourg
1448 returns to Mainz and begins printing the Bible
1450 goes into partnership with Johann Fust
1455 Fust takes Gutenberg to court and is given printing press as payment of the debt
1456 Fust completes printing Gutenberg Bible
1468 Gutenberg dies

6

James *Watt*

Father of the steam-engine

In 1764, when James Watt was a scientific instrument-maker at Glasgow University, Scotland, he was asked to repair a model of a steam-engine. The model was a type of engine designed in about 1712 by an English engineer, Thomas Newcomen. The Newcomen engine was used to pump water from mines and prevent them from flooding. Watt noticed that the engine had several design faults that made it very inefficient. He therefore decided to design a better steam-engine.

The steam-engine was invented by Thomas Newcomen, but James Watt made it much more efficient. It was needed for pumping out mines and stopping them from becoming flooded. The diagram shows Watt's double-acting steam-engine.

Watt went on to invent a rotative steam engine to provide power for the mills and factories that were being built all over Britain. Until the invention of this kind of steam-engine, factories were powered mainly by water turning a water-wheel or horses walking round a circular track.

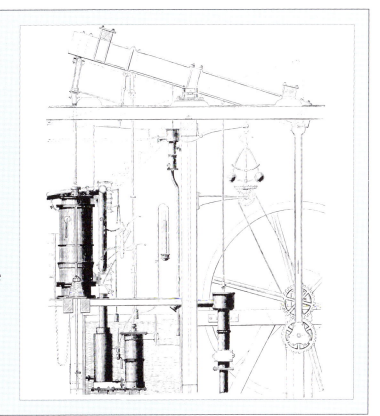

The Newcomen engine was very expensive to run because it used a great deal of coal. The coal was burned to heat water and turn it into steam. Like all steam-engines, the Newcomen engine worked on the principle that steam occupies much more space than the water from which it comes. When water is turned into steam in an enclosed space such as a boiler, it expands and produces a force that can be used to move parts of the steam-engine. In the Newcomen engine, steam was let into a cylinder beneath a piston, which moved a wooden beam attached to the pump below in the mine. The pressure of the steam forced the piston to the top of the cylinder. The steam was then condensed (turned back into water) with a spray of cold water, creating a partial vacuum that forced the piston down again. This downward motion worked the pump. Then more steam was let in, and the whole movement was repeated. The main problem with this system was that spraying cold water into the cylinder cooled down the cylinder itself, as well as the steam. This meant that the cylinder had to be heated again the next time steam was fed in. This constant reheating wasted energy.

Watt had the idea of turning the steam back to water – or condensing it – in a separate container instead of in the cylinder, so that the cylinder would always remain hot. He built a model of his separate-condenser engine and discovered that this idea worked. The steam was fed from the cylinder into the chamber until it had all condensed, while the cylinder remained hot.

In 1774, Watt went into partnership with Matthew Boulton, a manufacturer in Birmingham, England. The engines proved highly successful at pumping water from mines, especially in Cornwall where there were many tin and copper mines that were at risk from flooding. In 1781, Watt improved his engine by making the cylinder 'double-acting'. His first engines – like those of Newcomen – had supplied power on the down stroke only, when the piston was forced downward inside the cylinder. In his double-acting engine, steam was allowed into the cylinder and condensed first on one side of the piston and then on the other, so that power was produced on both the up and down strokes. This innovation almost doubled the power of his engines.

During this time, the Industrial Revolution was in full swing, and the factories and mills that were being built all over the country needed power to drive their machinery. But they needed rotary power to turn a central shaft round and

Matthew Boulton's factory in Birmingham. Watt built his first commercial steam-engines there.

round. This rotary motion, which was provided by horses walking around a circular track or the force of water to turn water-wheels, was then transferred to the factory machinery through a series of gears. Watt's engines, with their up-and-down motion, were good at pumping water out of mines but were of little use for driving factory machinery. After much persuasion by Boulton, Watt developed a rotative steam-engine that was soon put to use in factories and mills throughout the country.

Watt and Boulton needed a unit of measurement that would enable them to set the price of their steam-engines based on the rate at which an engine could work. Watt calculated that a horse being used to supply power in a mill could lift 33,000 pounds (15,000 kg) by 1 foot (0.305 m) in 1 minute. This became the standard measurement of 1 horsepower, and Watt described the power of his steam-engines in terms of how much horsepower they could supply.

A portrait of Watt, painted after he became famous.

Dates

1736 born in Greenock, Scotland
1754 starts training as a scientific instrument-maker
1763 studies and repairs model Newcomen steam-engine
1765 devises a separate-condenser engine
1776 builds a full-sized steam-engine
1777 begins building mine-pumping engines in Cornwall
1781 designs an engine with double-acting cylinder
1783 defines horsepower; constructs first rotative engine
1819 dies at Heathfield, near Birmingham

Louis *Daguerre*

Photographic pioneer

Louis Daguerre invented the Daguerreotype process, which was the first practical way of taking a photograph. He improved on earlier methods of taking photographs, which had been very slow. With the help of Joseph Nicéphore Niépce, he found a way of taking a photograph by pointing the camera at a scene for less than half an hour instead of the eight hours it had taken before.

The camera shown above was used for taking Daguerreotype pictures.

In the 1820s, Louis Daguerre was a painter, employed to paint stage sets at the opera theatre in Paris, France. He became fascinated by a popular device known as the camera obscura. This apparatus, invented by the Arabs around AD 900, consisted of a box with a small hole in the top. Sunlight entered through the hole and was then projected on to a screen to produce an image of the scene outside.

The 'picture' produced by the camera obscura was not permanent; it disappeared when the hole was covered and left no lasting image. Daguerre wanted to find a way to make the image permanent, and he set about producing what he called a 'heliographic picture'. He experimented with many different methods but without having any success. So, in 1829 he decided to team up with another Frenchman, Joseph Nicéphore Niépce, who had made the first-ever permanent photograph two years earlier.

Niépce's photographs were taken on a plate made of pewter, which was polished and then coated with bitumen (a type of asphalt) dissolved in white petroleum. The plate was positioned in a simple camera, which was then pointed towards the subject. Light entering the camera struck the plate and hardened the bitumen, bleaching it white. The more light reaching a part of the plate, the whiter that part became. The unhardened areas were then cleaned and darkened to improve the contrast with the white areas.

(Left)   Louis Daguerre (standing) and his partner, Joseph Niépce.
(Below)   This photograph, taken by Niépce, is one of the world's oldest surviving photographs.

The problem with this method was that it took a long time. In Niépce's first successful photograph – a view from his study window – he aimed his camera at the view for eight hours. During that time, the sun moved around the subject and changed the position of shadows and highlights, which made the final image extremely fuzzy. This method was clearly useless for taking portraits – no one could be expected to sit still for eight hours!

Daguerre and Niépce worked together to find a better way of taking photographs until 1833, when Niépce died. Finally, six years later, Daguerre discovered a faster process that produced a permanent photograph – which he called a Daguerreotype – in about twenty minutes. He announced his invention in January 1839, but kept the details of his process secret for seven months. In August he revealed that he had used a copper sheet plated with silver and treated with iodine vapour to make it sensitive to light. After the sheet had been struck by light entering the camera, it was removed and put in mercury vapour to develop the image. The photograph was then treated with salt to make it permanent.

The Daguerreotype process was the first practical means of producing photographs. Over the years, improvements to this original process have made photography so much easier and simpler that it has become one of the most popular pastimes in the world today.

This very early photograph of Louis Daguerre was taken in 1845, six years after his invention of the Daguerreotype process.

Dates

1789 born in Cormeilles, France
1827 Niépce takes the first permanent photograph
1829 Daguerre enters partnership with Niépce
1833 Niépce dies
1839 Daguerre invents the first practical method of taking photographs
1851 dies

Gottlieb *Daimler*

Pioneer of the petrol engine

The motor car is the most widely used form of powered transport today. The first practical car was invented by Karl Benz, a German engineer. However, the most important part of the motor car – the engine – was pioneered by another German, Gottlieb Daimler.

Both Benz and Daimler were inspired by the Belgian-French inventor, Étienne Lenoir, who, in 1862, was the first person to fit an internal-combustion engine to a 'horseless carriage'. Lenoir's machine, with its large, spoked wheels, did indeed look rather like a carriage. It was also very heavy, and its

A photograph of Daimler, taken after he had become a successful car manufacturer.

gas-fuelled engine lacked power. Daimler – who knew Lenoir – realized that the gas engine would be suitable for driving factory machinery, but he did not believe it would be useful for transport.

From 1872, Daimler worked as a factory manager for the engineer Nikolaus Otto, who was developing a more practical gas-fuelled engine at his works. One day, Otto asked Daimler to investigate the possibility of using petrol as a fuel instead of gas. Daimler realized the wisdom of this idea, and in 1882 he left to set up a company of his own in the town of Cannstatt.

Within three years Daimler had developed a light, powerful petrol engine and had fitted it to a bicycle. He drove his machine – a forerunner of the modern motorcycle –

The world's first motorcycle, built by Daimler in 1885.

through the streets of Cannstatt, doubtless terrifying passersby. He next adapted his engine for use in a boat. Then in 1886, he built his first four-wheeled automobile, which had a top speed of 17 kph.

The following year, he formed the Daimler Motor Company, which began producing the first Mercedes car in 1901. The car

Towards the end of the last century, many engineers dreamed of producing engines to power carriages. In 1885, Gottlieb Daimler developed the first petrol-driven internal-combustion engine. He used it to power the world's first motorcycle. The following year Karl Benz tested the first practical motor car. Both men formed their own companies and began producing cars. Many years later the companies joined together to form the well-known Mercedes-Benz Company.

The picture shows Daimler's first petrol-driven four-wheel automobile, which was built in 1886.

Daimler (second from right) seated in one of his motor cars.

was named after the baby daughter of an Austrian businessman, Emil Jellinek, who had helped provide the money for Daimler's company. Meanwhile, the first practical car with a petrol-fuelled internal-combustion engine had been designed by Benz in 1885; by 1895 he was manufacturing cars in large numbers at his factory in Mannheim. Although Benz and Daimler never met, in 1926, twenty-six years after Daimler's death, their two companies joined forces and started producing the world-famous Mercedes-Benz.

Dates

1834 born in Schorndorf, Germany
1860 visits Étienne Lenoir's factory in Paris
1872 becomes factory manager for Nikolaus Otto, working on gas-fuelled engines
1882 leaves Otto to work on developing a petrol engine
1885 fits petrol engine to bicycle
1886 modifies his engine for use in a boat; builds his first petrol-driven car
1886 first public run of Daimler's petrol-driven car
1887 forms the Daimler Motor Company
1889 designs new two-cylinder engine, which is more powerful than those of his rivals
1900 dies in Cannstatt.
1901 first Mercedes car is produced at the Daimler factory in Cannstatt
1926 Daimler and Benz companies merge and begin producing Mercedes-Benz cars

Alexander Graham *Bell*

Inventor of the telephone

Because of his interest in helping deaf people to speak, Alexander Graham Bell studied speech and the ways in which sounds are made and heard. While he was working and experimenting on a telegraph system with his assistant Thomas Watson, he accidentally discovered the principle of the telephone.

Alexander Graham Bell was born in Edinburgh, Scotland, in 1847. When he finished his education he worked with his father, helping deaf people learn to speak. At the age of twenty-three he caught tuberculosis, and his family moved to Canada, where the climate was drier and better for his health. The following year Bell moved to Boston, in the USA, where he became Professor of Vocal Physiology at Boston University.

His work at Boston involved the study of sound, especially speech, and how it is made

Bell makes the first call using the new telephone link between New York and Chicago, USA, in October 1892.

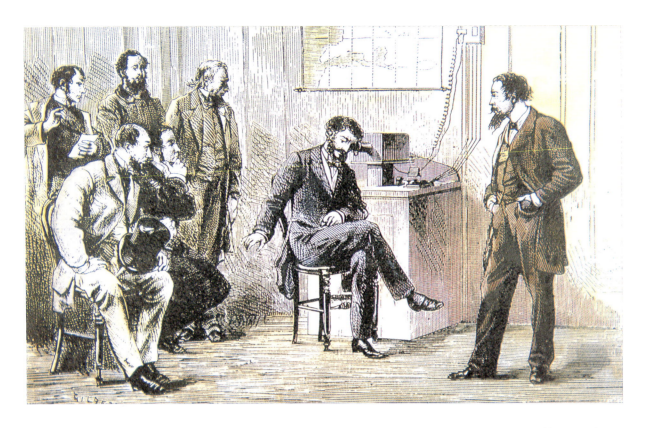

Bell's assistant, Thomas Watson, listens by telephone to Bell, who is speaking from a distance of 24 km.

and heard. In his spare time, Bell tried to develop a telegraph system that would allow the transmission (passing on) of several messages over one wire at the same time. Bell thought that this could be done by sending each message on a separate, specially tuned steel strip, or 'reed'. As each reed vibrated at a different speed, it would produce a different musical note.

It was while he was experimenting on this idea in 1875 that he made a great breakthrough – quite by accident. Bell and his assistant, Thomas Watson, were sitting in different rooms working on the telegraph equipment. When Bell sent a telegraph message to Watson's receiver, Watson noticed that one of the steel reeds failed to vibrate. He plucked the reed to make sure that it was not stuck, and this caused a reed in Bell's room to vibrate. Bell realized that the electric current produced by one vibrating reed was powerful enough to make another reed vibrate, even when the current had travelled along a wire from one room to another. He also realized that the reed had produced not one note, but several notes mixed together – just like human speech. He was convinced that he could use his system to send and receive the sound of a human voice.

Within a month, Bell made two simple telephones and, in the process, invented the first microphone. His telephone contained a reed that vibrated in response to sound waves caused by a human voice. The reed was next to an electromagnet, which turned the vibrations into an electric current. The current was sent along a wire to another telephone, which turned it back into sound by making an electromagnet vibrate a reed.

At first only mumbled sounds could be heard, but soon Bell was able to send a message that could be understood. The first words ever spoken on the telephone were heard by Bell's assistant in another room: 'Mr Watson, come here. I want to see you!'

In 1876 Bell took out a patent on his new invention. He arrived at the patent office just a few hours before another inventor, Elisha Gray, who had also come to patent an 'electrical speech machine' that he had devised quite separately. For the next ten years, the two men argued in courts about who had invented the telephone first. Eventually Bell won, and he became extremely wealthy soon after. He devoted the rest of his life to teaching deaf children.

The first telephone manufactured for the Post Office in Britain, in 1878.

Dates

1847 born in Edinburgh, Scotland
1870 moves to Canada
1871 moves to Boston, USA
1873 becomes Professor of Vocal Physiology
1875 discovers accidentally the principle of the telephone
1876 makes and patents first telephone; gives public demonstration in Philadelphia; first long-distant call made between Brantford and Paris, Canada, a distance of 100 km
1877 forms Bell Telephone Company
1892 opens New York to Chicago telephone line in USA
1922 dies in Nova Scotia, Canada

Thomas Alva *Edison*

An inventive genius

Thomas Edison invented more things than any other person and he was, without doubt, a genius. Yet, when he was at school in Milan, Ohio, in the USA, his teacher thought he was backward and perhaps slightly insane because of his strange and original ideas. On hearing this, Edison's mother took him out of school and taught him at home.

Edison probably produced more inventions than any other inventor the world has ever known. He took out patents on more than 1,300 devices. His most famous inventions include the phonograph (record player), an early form of the light bulb, an electricity generating system for lighting up towns, and the first talking pictures.

A portrait of Edison with his phonograph, painted in 1889.

In 1859, at the age of twelve, Edison got his first job, selling newspapers on the early-morning train between Port Huron and Detroit, Michigan. However, he was not content with just selling newspapers and soon started his own weekly journal, the *Grand Trunk Herald*, which he printed on an old printing press in the baggage car of the train. Later he worked as a telegraph operator and was always making improvements to the equipment. In 1869 he moved to New York, where he had a stroke of good fortune. One day, he happened to be visiting the Gold Indicator Company when the 'stock-ticker' machine that provided the prices of gold broke down. He fixed it on the spot and then devised his own machine, which he was able to sell for a great deal of money.

Edison used the money to set up a workshop in Newark, New Jersey, where he manufactured stock-ticker machines and continued to make improvements to telegraph machinery. Seven years later, he moved to Menlo Park and set about making an improved version of the telephone that had been invented by Alexander Graham Bell. Edison's system was very successful and he sold it in England.

In 1877, Edison produced the first version of his own favourite invention – the phonograph. This was an early

forerunner of the record player. Recordings were made by cutting grooves in the surface of a metal cylinder and played back by a needle running through grooves as the cylinder was turned round and round. The following year, he formed the Edison Electric Light Company. At that time, buildings and streets were lit by gas lamps, and Edison was determined to find a way of using electricity instead of gas. In order to achieve this he had to make an electric light bulb.

In 1860 an English scientist, Joseph Swan, had shown that when an electric current is passed through a thin thread, or filament, of carbonized paper, the filament becomes hot and gives off a bright light. To prevent the filament from burning away, he enclosed it in a glass bulb from which most of the air was removed, producing a partial vacuum. However, it was impossible at that time to remove all the air from the bulb, so the filament burnt out quite quickly. This problem was solved in 1865 with the invention of an effective vacuum pump, and Swan began work again on his light bulb. Finally, in January 1879, he demonstrated his invention. This was nine months before Edison achieved his first success – producing a light bulb that burned for nearly fourteen hours.

Nonetheless, it was Edison who made the headlines. On New Year's Eve 1879, a crowd of thirty thousand people gathered at Edison's laboratory in Menlo Park to see what the inventor had described as 'the eighth wonder of the world'. As it grew dark, Edison gave the order to switch on, and the laboratory and the street leading to it were lit up instantly by dozens of electric lights. Two years later, New York became the first city in the world to be lit by electric lights, using generators designed by Edison.

Edison did not believe in resting on his past achievements. He was constantly busy – often working twenty hours a day – and once remarked that 'Genius is one per cent inspiration and ninety-nine per cent perspiration.' From 1889, Edison became interested in motion pictures. He introduced a number of changes and set up his own film studios; in 1912 he produced the first talking motion picture. Edison continued to work on new ideas until his death in 1931, by which time he had taken out patents on almost 1,300 inventions.

A poster advertising the Edison Moving Picture Machine, an early cinema projector.

Dates

1847 born in Ohio, USA
1859 becomes a newsboy on a train and then produces his own paper
1864 works as telegraph operator and invents a transmitter capable of sending four telegraph messages at once
1871 invents new stock-ticker machine
1876 opens laboratory at Menlo Park, New Jersey
1877 invents the phonograph
1878 forms Edison Electric Light Company
1879 gives first 'illumination display' at Menlo Park
1882 New York illuminated by electric lights
1912 produces the first talking motion picture
1931 dies at West Orange, New Jersey

The *Wright* Brothers

Pioneers of aviation

Wilbur and Orville Wright pioneered the first flight of an aeroplane under its own power. On 17 December 1903, Orville took off in *Flyer I* at Kitty Hawk, North Carolina, in the USA. On that occasion the plane stayed in the air for only twelve seconds, but in 1905 Wilbur increased the time to 38 minutes, and in 1908 Orville flew for 75 minutes and travelled a distance of 124 km. This was the beginning of the age of flight.

Ever since the earliest time, humans have wanted to fly like birds. The first attempts to fly were in ornithopters, which were a type of aircraft designed to be propelled by the flapping of the wings. Ornithopters did not succeed simply because humans do not have the same structure of bones and muscles as birds. The first successful flight was in a hot-air balloon, built by the Montgolfier brothers.

It took to the air near Paris, France, in 1783, with two people on board. The earliest flight in a winged aircraft came in 1851, when a glider – an aircraft with no engine – carried a man a short distance through the air.

At that time, steam-engines were used to power ships and drive factory machinery. Some people tried fitting gliders with steam-engines, but they were far too heavy. The first powered aircraft flight had to wait for the invention of the internal-combustion engine, which was pioneered by Gottlieb Daimler in 1885.

In 1896 Wilbur and Orville Wright, who ran a bicycle repair shop in Dayton, Ohio, USA, read about Otto Lilienthal,

25

a German engineer who experimented with gliders. Lilienthal's exploits fired the brothers' imagination, and they became determined to build a machine that could fly. In 1899 they began experimenting with large kites and gliders. First they looked for a place where the weather conditions were suitable for their tests. From a list supplied by the US Weather Bureau the Wright brothers chose an area of coastal sand-dunes near Kitty Hawk, North Carolina.

The Wright brothers built three gliders, and by 1903 they had carried out more than a thousand glides, sometimes in winds of up to 56 kph. When they were satisfied that their

One of the Wright brothers' planes being transported on a trailer pulled by a car in 1903.

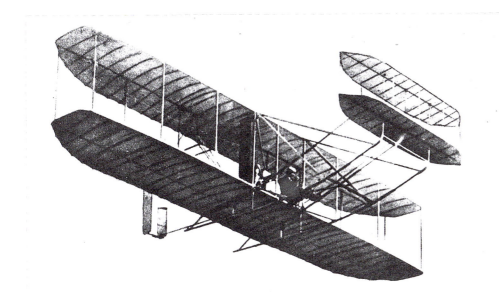

One of the first military aircraft, built by the Wright brothers for the US Army.

glider design worked well, they began to think about attaching an engine. Like others before them, they found that all the engines available were too heavy, so they designed and built their own petrol engine. They also designed two efficient propellers. The Wright brothers were now ready to fly.

On 17 December 1903, Orville climbed aboard the plane, named *Flyer I*. It slid down the slope on its ski-like undercarriage, and its propellers lifted it 3 m up into the air. Although the plane stayed in the air for just 12 seconds, powered flight had become a reality and the Wright brothers had made history.

The brothers made three more flights that day, the longest of which lasted 59 seconds and covered a distance of 284 m. They soon built more powerful planes, and in 1909 they were asked to build the first military aircraft. In the same year they set up their own aircraft factory and flying school in Dayton.

Dates

1867 Wilbur Wright born in Dayton, Ohio, USA
1871 Orville born in Dayton
1892 open a bicycle repair shop in Dayton
1899 begin experiments with large kites
1900 start experimenting with gliders
1903 Orville makes world's first powered flight in *Flyer I*
1908 Orville demonstrates *Flyer II* in USA and is airborne for 1 hour, 15 minutes
1909 they build military planes; set up an aircraft factory and flying school in Dayton
1912 Wilbur dies in Millville, Indiana, USA
1948 Orville dies in Dayton

Guglielmo *Marconi*

Inventor of wireless telegraphy

The wireless telegraph invented by Guglielmo Marconi sent dot-dash (Morse code) signals through the air by radio waves instead of over a wire. His 'wireless' invention led to the development of radio, and later to the modern radio communication system that is now used all over the world.

In 1894, the twenty-year-old Guglielmo Marconi heard about the work of a German scientist, Heinrich Hertz. Some years earlier, Hertz had shown that there are invisible waves – called electromagnetic waves – that travel through space at about 300,000 km a second. (We now know that light, ultraviolet rays, X-rays and microwaves are all examples of electromagnetic waves.)

Hertz's work fascinated Marconi, who believed that these waves could be used to send messages over long distances without

Marconi in 1901, photographed with transmitting and receiving equipment similar to that which sent the first radio signal across the Atlantic.

A *radio receiver built by Marconi in 1897.*

wires. He set up a workshop in the attic of his parents' house near Bologna, Italy, and began experimenting. He used various pieces of equipment invented by other people and soon succeeded in making a bell ring by sending a 'wireless' (or radio) signal across the room. Less than a year later, he managed to increase the range of his apparatus so that it could send a dot-and-dash signal like those used in the telegraph over a distance of 3 km.

Marconi then tried to find someone who would provide the money needed to develop his system of 'wireless telegraphy'. But no one in Italy was willing to invest money; not even the Italian Ministry of Posts and Telegraph was interested. They failed to see the advantages of Marconi's wireless telegraph over their telegraph system, which could work only if the transmitter and receiver were connected by wires. Marconi was bitterly disappointed and decided to move to England, where his mother had friends. He applied for a British patent for his invention and later demonstrated its usefulness to officials from the Post Office in London by sending signals between two buildings 300 m apart. Shortly afterwards, he was asked to give another demonstration to army and navy officers on Salisbury Plain, and he succeeded in transmitting signals over 6 km.

By 1897, Marconi was able to send signals over a distance of 19 km. Two years later, the first messages were sent across the English Channel to France. Then, in 1901, as a result of improvements made by Marconi to his apparatus, the first transatlantic radio signal was sent. It was transmitted from Poldhu in Cornwall, England, and received by Marconi himself in St John's, Newfoundland, in Canada. After this, Marconi's invention began to be used by ships as a way of communicating.

Marconi (wearing cap) and a wireless operator in the receiving room at Glace Bay, Nova Scotia, Canada.

Dates

1874 born in Bologna, Italy
1894 begins to experiment with radio waves
1895 succeeds in transmitting radio messages over a distance of 3 km
1896 moves to London, England, and successfully demonstrates his wireless apparatus
1897 forms The Wireless Telegraph and Signal Company, later re-named The Marconi Company
1899 sends a signal across the English Channel to France
1901 receives first radio signals sent across the Atlantic
1906 first radio broadcast of speech in USA
1920 The Marconi Company broadcasts first British radio programme
1922 the BBC is founded
1937 dies in Rome, Italy

These early signals were all in the form of Morse code – dots and dashes – but in 1906 the world's first radio broadcast of speech was made in Massachusetts, USA. Marconi was interested in the use of wireless more for communication purposes than for popular radio broadcasting, and he worked on what we now call 'very high frequency' (VHF) transmissions and on so-called short-wave radio. Nonetheless, he was a businessman as well as an inventor, and he realized that radio could become very popular with the public. Therefore, in 1920 his company broadcast the first British radio programme. Two years later, the British Broadcasting Corporation (BBC) was formed and started transmitting regular radio programmes in 1927.

Robert *Goddard*

Father of the space rocket

Robert Goddard invented the liquid-fuelled rocket. He built and launched rockets that could reach tremendous speeds and heights, but it was many years before people realized the importance of his work. Since the 1950s, Goddard's rocketry inventions have helped to make moon landings and many other space missions possible.

As a teenager, Goddard was fascinated by rockets, which had been used by the Chinese in warfare since about AD 1200, and in Europe from around 1800. However, Goddard was interested in building rockets not as weapons but as a means of travelling to the moon or another planet.

In 1914, when Goddard was thirty-two, he became a physics teacher at Clark University in his home town of Worcester, Massachusetts, in the USA. Shortly afterwards, he patented two rocket devices and wrote a text-book

Goddard lecturing to students at Clark University in 1924.

called *A Method of Reaching Extreme Altitudes*. In the book, Goddard suggested ways of reaching the moon with a multi-stage rocket.

In the 1920s, Goddard began experimenting with liquid-fuelled rockets. Until then, rockets had been propelled by gunpowder. Goddard hoped his new type of rocket would be powerful enough to reach the 'extreme altitudes' he had predicted. In 1926 he launched the world's first liquid-fuelled rocket. It consisted of a metal tubing about 3 m long with a motor and nozzle attached at the top. When the fuel was set alight, exhaust gases shot out through the nozzle. The rocket rose just over 12 m into the air and crashed 56 m away. In 1929, Goddard launched a much larger rocket that was the first to carry instruments such as a thermometer, barometer and small camera. However, his new rocket was so noisy that people complained to the police, and he was ordered not to fire any more rockets in the state of Massachusetts. Partly because of this, he was not given any government backing or funds to continue his work.

Goddard experimenting with an early type of bazooka – a weapon that fires a rocket-propelled projectile.

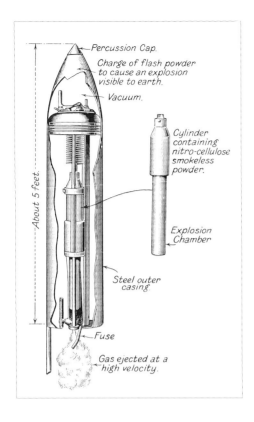

A diagram showing one of Goddard's first rockets, designed in 1924.

One person who was interested in Goddard's work was the famous aviator Charles Lindbergh, who in 1927 had made the first solo flight across the Atlantic Ocean. Lindberg persuaded the American industrialist Daniel Guggenheim to grant Goddard $50,000 to continue his rocket research. Goddard used this money to set up a rocket-testing station in New Mexico, where he built and launched rockets that reached speeds of up to 800 kph and heights of up to 2.4 km. In 1935 he became the first person to fire a liquid-fuelled rocket faster than the speed of sound, which is almost 1,200 kph.

In all, Goddard took out more than two hundred rocket patents. Some of them covered inventions that were ahead of their time, and years passed before people understood how important they were. They included scientific breakthroughs that helped to make possible the 1969 American moon landing and many other space missions.

Goddard (second from right) and his assistants prepare to test fire a rocket at the testing station in New Mexico, USA, in 1931.

The launch of a space shuttle. Modern rockets like this are based on the pioneering work of Robert Goddard.

Dates

1882 born in Worcester, Massachusetts, USA
1914 becomes physics teacher at Clark University, Worcester
1919 publishes *A Method of Reaching Extreme Altitudes*
1926 carries out first tests on liquid-fuelled rockets
1929 fires rocket carrying scientific instruments and camera
1930 receives grant from Guggenheim Foundation and sets up rocket-testing station in New Mexico, USA
1935 fires rocket faster than the speed of sound
1945 dies in Annapolis, Maryland, USA

Sadly, during his lifetime, Goddard and his achievements were ignored by the United States government. Finally, in 1960, fifteen years after Goddard died, the government realized the value of his work and paid $1 million to use his patents. Robert Goddard is now recognized as the father of the space rocket.

John Logie *Baird*

Pioneer of television

John Logie Baird developed the world's first television set. In 1929 he demonstrated his invention by televising a ventriloquist's dummy. The flickering black-and-white figure on the screen was a great success and Baird became famous. Meanwhile two other British companies were also working on their own television system, which proved to be more practical, and Baird's system was abandoned. Although his invention was not a success, Baird is famous as the man who invented television.

John Logie Baird studied electrical engineering at Glasgow University and worked as an engineer for the Clyde Valley electric power company. However, he suffered from poor health and in 1922, at the age of thirty-four, he was forced to give up work and move to Hastings, England, where the climate was warmer than in his native Scotland.

One day in 1923, Baird was taking a walk along the cliffs near Hastings. As he walked, he thought about radio, which had been pioneered by Guglielmo Marconi some years before. Suddenly, an idea came to him. If we can hear by radio, it should be possible to see by radio, too. By the end of his walk, Baird had worked out a method of sending pictures using radio waves.

He set to work collecting all of the parts he thought he would need. Some were old radio components; others were bits and pieces he got from local scrapyards. Eventually he built a clumsy contraption and tried it out. He managed to produce a flickering image on a white screen positioned behind his apparatus.

Baird borrowed some money to improve his equipment and rented an attic workshop in Soho, London. It was there, in 1926, that he gave the first public demonstration of what he called 'seeing by wireless' – television. The black-and-white image that appeared on the

Baird working on his early television equipment.

screen was the face of a ventriloquist's dummy, and the audience – members of the Royal Institution – were greatly impressed.

Almost overnight, Baird became famous. He set up his own company and started to improve the quality of his pictures. Within two years he also produced the first-ever colour television pictures, although they were of very poor quality. In 1929, he persuaded the British Broadcasting Corporation (which had been founded in 1922 to broadcast radio programmes) to begin transmitting a daily black-and-white television service. The pictures were sent from Baird's own TV studio – the world's first – using a radio transmitter lent to him by the BBC. The following year, the BBC lent him a second transmitter so that he could send sound with his pictures.

Meanwhile, other inventors were working on their own ideas to improve the quality of TV pictures. Two British Companies – Electrical Musical Industries (EMI) and The Marconi Company – teamed up in 1934 to develop an electronic TV system.

This was very different from Baird's system because it used electronic components both in the camera that took the TV pictures and in the television set that received them. Baird relied on mechanical parts for his camera and television apparatus, and his system was soon

Baird's original television apparatus. The ventriloquist's dummy that he used in his first TV demonstration is marked 'A' in the picture.

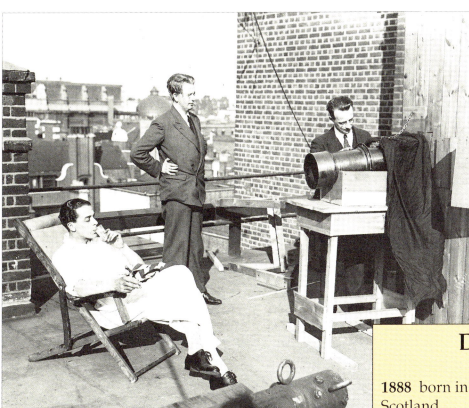

Baird (on the right) prepares to broadcast black-and-white television pictures from the roof of his studio in 1929.

seen to have disadvantages. For instance, his cameras had to be bolted to the floor because of the speed at which the machinery turned inside. The electronic system was much more practical and gave a clearer picture than Baird's mechanical television.

Nonetheless, when the BBC began the world's first public TV broadcasts in November 1936, they used both systems alternately – Baird's system one week and the Marconi-EMI system the next. Within three months the Marconi-EMI system showed its superiority, and Baird's mechanical television was abandoned forever. The inventor of television was ruined, and he remained sad and bitter about the BBC's decision for the rest of his life.

Wallace *Carothers*

Inventor of nylon

Until Wallace Carothers invented the strong, light fibre called nylon, all textiles were made completely or mainly from natural products. He wanted to produce an artificial fibre that would look as much like silk as possible. His synthetic fibre, made in a laboratory, was strong, light, hardwearing, cheap to produce, and proved to have endless uses.

In 1935, Wallace Carothers was Director of Research at the du Pont chemical company in the USA, where he was attempting to develop an artificial fibre with the same properties as silk. Silk is a natural fibre obtained from the cocoons of silkworms, which are cultivated especially for that purpose. Until the 1940s,

Carothers in his laboratory at the du Pont chemical company.

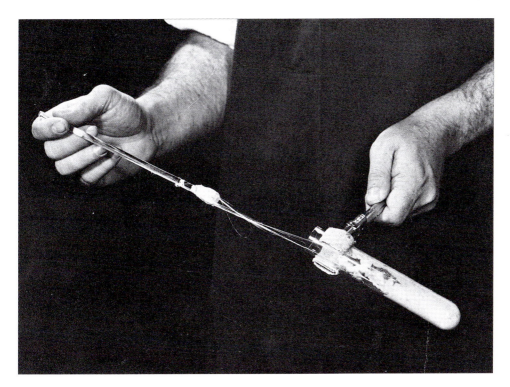

The molecules that make up nylon are in the form of long chains and the material can easily be spun into fibres.

most high-quality silk came from China (where silk production first began) and from Japan. Because of its luxurious look and feel, silk has for centuries been used for making clothes, but its main drawback is that it is very expensive to produce.

As long ago as 1884, the French chemist Hilaire Chardonnet had made an artificial silk fibre called rayon, using cellulose, a substance made from plants. Chardonnet's process involved the use of a highly inflammable substance that was dangerous to work with, but later improvements made rayon much safer to manufacture. However, cellulose was a natural substance; Carothers wanted to do what no one else had managed to do – invent a totally artificial fibre that was superior to rayon, looked and felt as much like silk as possible, but cost much less to manufacture.

After a great deal of research, Carothers and his team succeeded. They produced a substance known as polyamide 6,6, which

Life-saving parachutes are manufactured from nylon.

Nylon is often used to make mechanical components, like the large gear-wheel inside this chainsaw.

consists of long chains of molecules. The molecules of polyamide 6,6 are joined together in a similar way to those in natural silk, and can easily be spun to make fibres. Carother's company, du Pont, were excited by the possibilities for their new fibre and by the fact that it was completely artificial (unlike rayon), which meant it would not rot or be eaten by insects. Polyamide 6,6 was about to be put on to the market with the name duproh, short for 'du Pont pulls rabbit out of hat', but was renamed nylon just before the launch.

Nylon was an instant success. It was first used to make bristles for toothbrushes, and then clothing, ropes, engine parts, furnishing fabrics, parachutes, and much more. Sadly, Carothers did not live to enjoy his success. He suffered from a form of a mental illness known as depression. Even though he had proved himself a brilliant chemist, when he was depressed he believed he was a failure. In 1937, while suffering from depression, he killed himself.

Dates

1896 born in Burlington, Ohio, USA

1928 starts work for du Pont chemical company

1935 succeeds in making the first artificial fibre, polyamide 6,6; his invention is patented by du Pont

1937 commits suicide in Philadelphia, USA

1938 Polyamide 6,6 is first sold by du Pont under the name nylon and is used to make toothbrush bristles

Frank *Whittle*

Pioneer of jet propulsion

All modern jet aircraft are powered by engines based on the first jet engine. This was developed by Frank Whittle in 1937. A jet engine pushes the aircraft forward by shooting out a stream, or jet, of gas from the rear of the engine. Whittle's invention meant that aircraft could travel very much faster. Further developments enabled jet aircraft to fly much higher and carry many more passengers.

In 1923, Frank Whittle joined the Royal Air Force (RAF) and five years later became a fighter pilot. In those days, aircraft were driven by propellers turned by internal-combustion engines, similar to those in motor cars. These engines were not powerful enough to enable planes to fly very far or at high altitudes.

Whittle thought that he could design a much more powerful type of engine. His idea was to thrust an aircraft forward through the air by forcing out a jet of gas backwards from the plane's engine. Air would be sucked into the front of the engine, then heated and squeezed, or 'compressed', by a fan.

Frank Whittle working at his desk.

This Gloster E28/39 *was the first aircraft to be propelled by Whittle's jet engine.*

Concorde *takes off over the landing lights at Heathrow Airport, England. Modern jet engines are much more powerful than those built by Whittle but they are based on his designs.*

The compressed air would then be mixed with a fuel called kerosene and set alight. This would cause the air to expand and rush out through the back of the engine. On its way, the expanded air would turn a turbine connected to the compressor fan at the front of the engine, causing that to turn, too. The air surging from the rear of the engine would push the plane forward. You can see this effect if you blow up a balloon, let it go and watch it fly around; Whittle's engine was basically a much more complicated version.

In 1928, shortly after he graduated as an officer from the RAF College at Cranwell, Whittle published his ideas for using jet propulsion to power aircraft. Two years later, he took out his first jet engine patent. In 1937 – after studying for three years at Cambridge

University to gain more technical knowledge – he built a prototype engine that worked well in tests in a laboratory. Even so, Whittle had great difficulty in persuading anyone that his invention would be useful, and it was not until 1941 that the engine was first used to power an aeroplane – a *Gloster E28/39*.

This was not the first jet flight, however. In Germany, Dr Hans von Ohain had been working independently on jet propulsion, and, in 1939, a *Heinkel He178* plane took to the air powered by his jet engines. Nonetheless, it was Whittle's design that was used as the basis for later engines, and all modern jet aircraft rely on engines that have been developed from his original ideas. Frank Whittle was knighted in 1948 and now lives in retirement in England.

Dates

1907 born in Coventry, England
1923 joins RAF
1928 graduates from Cranwell College as RAF Officer; publishes ideas on jet propulsion
1934 becomes student at Cambridge University
1937 graduates from Cambridge; successfully tests jet engine in laboratory
1939 German aircraft becomes first to fly with jet engine
1941 first flight of Whittle's jet engine
1949 flight of world's first jet airliner, De Havilland *Comet*

Sir Frank Whittle in 1988, with a modern Rolls-Royce jet engine and one of his own engines of the 1940s.

Glossary

Antimony   A type of metal often used in making alloys (mixtures of metals).

Artificial   Something that is produced by humans and does not occur naturally.

Barometer   An instrument for measuring atmospheric pressure.

Components   Parts of something. For example, a turbine is a component of a jet engine.

Cylinder   The part of an engine in which a piston is forced backwards and forwards by steam or burning fuel.

Electromagnet   A magnet consisting of a piece of iron or steel with wire wound around it. It becomes a magnet only when an electric current is passed through the wire.

Electronic   Having to do with electrons, tiny particles that are charged with electricity.

Filament   The thin wire inside a light bulb that gives out light when heated by an electric current.

Generator   An apparatus for producing electricity.

Inflammable   Easily set on fire.

Internal-combustion engine   An engine that is driven by burning fuel (such as petrol) inside a cylinder. The burning of the fuel forces a piston to move, driving the moving parts of the machine (for example, a car) to which the engine is attached.

Mint   A place where money is manufactured by the authority of a government.

Molecules   Two or more atoms joined together. Atoms are the tiny building blocks from which all things are made.

Morse code   An international code used for sending messages, originally by telegraph. Letters and numbers are represented by dots and dashes.

Patent   A permit from a government, giving an inventor the sole right to make, use and sell his or her invention.

Pewter   An alloy, or mixture of metals, containing tin and lead, sometimes with small quantities of other metals such as antimony and copper.

Piston   A type of plunger that moves backwards and forwards inside the cylinder of an engine, compressing the steam or fuel inside.

Prototype   An early version of something, made so that tests can be carried out on it and improvements can be made to the design.

Receiver   A device for picking up sound or radio waves. Examples include radio and television sets.

Rotative   Causing rotation, or spin.

Royal Institution A society founded in Britain in 1799 to spread scientific knowledge.

Telegraph A device for sending messages over distances by passing electrical signals along a wire.

Transmitter A device for sending out sound or radio waves.

Tuberculosis A disease, usually affecting the lungs, that causes coughing and makes it difficult for a sufferer to breathe.

Turbine A wheel that is made to spin at high speed by a powerful flow of water, a jet of steam or expanding hot air.

Vacuum A space that contains air at very low pressure. It is impossible to create a total vacuum in which the pressure is zero.

Books to read

Alexander Graham Bell by Andrew Dunn (Wayland, 1990)

The Book of Inventions and Discoveries edited by Valérie-Anne Giscard d'Estaing (Macdonald Queen Anne Press, 1991)

Thomas Edison by Nina Morgan (Wayland, 1991)

Invention by Lionel Bender (Dorling Kindersley, 1991)

Inventions by Peter Turvey (Franklin Watts, 1991)

Inventions that Changed the World (Readers Digest, 1982)

Guglielmo Marconi by Nina Morgan (Wayland, 1990)

Usborne Illustrated Handbook of Invention and Discovery by Struan Reid (Usborne, 1986)

James Watt by Douglas McTavish (Wayland, 1992)

Index